The Future of Data: Exploring Blockchain's Role in Secure Storage and Sharing

Salinger

Author: Salinger

Title: The Future of Data: Exploring Blockchain's Role in Secure Storage and Sharing

This book is a product of [Publisher's Salinger]

ISBN:

TABLE OF CONTENTS

Chapter 1: Introduction to Blockchain Technology

Understanding Blockchain Technology

Blockchain technology is revolutionizing the way data is stored and shared in today's digital world. It has the potential to transform various industries, including finance, supply chain management, healthcare, and more. In this subchapter, we will explore the fundamentals of blockchain technology and its significant role in secure storage and sharing of data.

At its core, a blockchain is a decentralized and distributed ledger that records transactions across multiple computers or nodes. Each transaction is grouped into a block and added to the chain in a chronological order, creating an immutable and transparent record of all activities. This decentralized nature eliminates the need for intermediaries, such as banks or third-party service providers, resulting in faster and more efficient transactions.

One of the key features of blockchain technology is its enhanced security. Each block in the chain is cryptographically linked to the previous block, creating a chain of trust that ensures the integrity of the data stored within. Moreover, the distributed nature of the blockchain makes it highly resistant to hacking or data manipulation, as altering a single block would require modifying the entire chain across multiple nodes simultaneously.

Blockchain technology also offers transparency and accountability. As all transactions are recorded on the blockchain and visible to all participants, it promotes trust and eliminates the need for audits or third-party verification. This transparency makes it an ideal solution for industries such as supply chain management, where stakeholders can track the movement of goods from their origin to the final destination, ensuring authenticity and quality.

Furthermore, blockchain technology enables the creation of smart contracts, which are self-executing contracts with predefined rules encoded within the blockchain. These smart contracts automate processes, eliminate the need for intermediaries, and ensure the accurate execution of agreements, saving time and reducing costs.

In addition to its security and transparency benefits, blockchain technology also addresses the issue of data privacy. With traditional centralized systems, individuals have limited control over their data, exposing them to potential breaches or misuse. However, blockchain technology allows individuals to have ownership and control over their data, granting permission-based access to third parties and ensuring privacy.

In conclusion, blockchain technology is a game-changer in the digital era. Its decentralized nature, enhanced security, transparency, and privacy features make it a powerful tool for secure storage and sharing of data. As blockchain continues to evolve, it has the potential to transform various industries, creating a more efficient, transparent, and secure future for all. Whether you are a technology enthusiast, a business professional, or simply curious about the blockchain revolution, understanding this transformative technology is essential for everyone.

Historical Background of Blockchain

Blockchain technology has gained immense popularity and recognition in recent years, but its origins can be traced back to a much earlier time. To truly understand the potential and impact of blockchain, it is essential to delve into its historical background.

The concept of blockchain was first introduced in a whitepaper published in 2008 by an individual or group of individuals using the pseudonym Satoshi Nakamoto. This whitepaper outlined the foundation of Bitcoin, the first decentralized digital currency. Bitcoin, which operates on blockchain technology, was a breakthrough in the world of finance and digital transactions.

However, the roots of blockchain can be traced back even further. The fundamental concept of a distributed ledger, which forms the basis of blockchain, can be found in the work of Stuart Haber and W. Scott Stornetta in 1991. They proposed a system to timestamp digital documents using cryptographic methods, ensuring immutability and tamper resistance.

The true historical background of blockchain, however, lies in the pursuit of trusted digital transactions. Early attempts to create digital currencies faced challenges in achieving trust and preventing double-spending. The introduction of blockchain technology provided a solution to these problems by facilitating secure and transparent transactions without the need for intermediaries.

The historical background of blockchain also includes the development of various blockchain platforms and projects. Ethereum, launched in 2015, introduced the concept of smart contracts, enabling the execution of programmable transactions without the need for third-party intermediaries. This further expanded the potential applications of blockchain beyond financial transactions.

Over time, blockchain technology has captured the attention of not only the financial sector but also various industries, including supply chain management, healthcare, and even governance. Its ability to provide secure, transparent, and decentralized solutions has made it a revolutionary force.

In summary, the historical background of blockchain showcases the evolution of a technology that has the potential to transform the way we store and share data securely. From its inception with Bitcoin to the development of smart contracts, blockchain has come a long way. By understanding its historical roots, we can better appreciate the immense potential and possibilities that blockchain offers for the future of data storage and sharing.

This subchapter aims to provide a comprehensive overview of the historical background of blockchain for readers from all walks of life. Whether you are new to blockchain or have some knowledge in the field, this subchapter will equip you with the necessary understanding of its origins and evolution. Explore the historical background of blockchain and embark on a journey to discover its role in secure storage and sharing.

Key Concepts and Components of Blockchain

In recent years, blockchain technology has emerged as a revolutionary force in the realm of data storage and sharing. Its decentralized and transparent nature has the potential to disrupt various industries and redefine the way we interact with digital information. To truly grasp the power of blockchain, it is crucial to understand its key concepts and components.

At its core, blockchain is a distributed ledger that records transactions across multiple computers or nodes. These transactions are grouped into blocks, which are then linked using cryptographic hashes to form an immutable chain. This decentralized structure ensures that no single entity has control over the network, making it resistant to tampering and hacking.

One of the fundamental concepts of blockchain is transparency. Every transaction added to the blockchain is visible to all participants, creating a high level of trust and accountability. This transparency is achieved through consensus mechanisms, such as proof of work or proof of stake, where participants validate and verify transactions before they are added to the chain.

Another key concept is security. Blockchain employs advanced cryptographic techniques to secure data and prevent unauthorized access. Each block contains a unique hash, which is a digital fingerprint of the data it holds. Any alteration to the data would result in a different hash, alerting the network of potential tampering. Additionally, the distributed nature of blockchain makes it highly resilient to attacks, as compromising a single node would have minimal impact on the overall network.

The components of a blockchain network include nodes, blocks, and smart contracts. Nodes are individual computers or devices that participate in the network by storing a copy of the blockchain and validating transactions. Blocks, as mentioned earlier, are containers of transactions that form the chain. Smart contracts, on the other hand, are self-executing contracts with predefined rules encoded on the blockchain. They automate processes and eliminate the need for intermediaries, reducing costs and increasing efficiency.

For EVERYONE interested in blockchain, understanding these key concepts and components is essential. Whether you are a technology enthusiast, a business owner, or a curious individual, grasping the fundamentals of blockchain will empower you to explore its potential applications and make informed decisions.

In conclusion, blockchain is a revolutionary technology that has the potential to transform the way we store and share data securely. By embracing transparency, security, and decentralization, blockchain has emerged as a powerful tool for various industries. Understanding the key concepts and components of blockchain is the first step towards harnessing its potential and shaping the future of data.

Benefits and Limitations of Blockchain

Blockchain technology has garnered significant attention in recent years for its potential to revolutionize various industries, including finance, healthcare, supply chain management, and more. As we explore the future of data and the role blockchain plays in secure storage and sharing, it is essential to understand the benefits and limitations of this groundbreaking technology.

One of the most significant advantages of blockchain is its ability to provide enhanced security. Traditional data storage methods often rely on a centralized authority, making them vulnerable to hacking and data breaches. However, blockchain operates on a decentralized network, where data is stored across multiple nodes, ensuring that no single point of failure exists. This decentralized nature makes it extremely difficult for hackers to manipulate or corrupt data, enhancing the overall security and integrity of stored information.

Another key benefit of blockchain is its transparency and immutability. Every transaction recorded on the blockchain is visible to all participants in the network, creating a transparent and accountable environment. This feature is particularly valuable in industries that require trust and verification, such as supply chain management or financial transactions. Additionally, once a transaction is recorded on the blockchain, it becomes nearly impossible to alter or delete, ensuring the integrity and immutability of data.

Blockchain also offers increased efficiency and cost-effectiveness. By eliminating intermediaries and streamlining processes, blockchain reduces the need for manual verification and reconciliation, ultimately saving time and resources. Smart contracts, a feature of blockchain technology, enable automated and self-executing agreements, further streamlining operations and reducing costs.

However, despite its numerous benefits, blockchain also has certain limitations that must be considered. Firstly, scalability remains a challenge for blockchain networks. As more transactions are added to the chain, the network can become slower and less efficient. Additionally, the energy consumption associated with blockchain mining, especially in the case of proof-of-work consensus algorithms, raises environmental concerns.

Furthermore, blockchain technology is still in its early stages of development, and widespread adoption is yet to be achieved. Integration with existing systems and regulatory frameworks poses challenges, requiring comprehensive education and collaboration between various stakeholders.

In conclusion, blockchain holds tremendous potential for secure data storage and sharing. Its decentralized nature, enhanced security, transparency, and efficiency make it an attractive solution for various industries. However, scalability and regulatory challenges, as well as the need for further development and education, should be acknowledged. As the future unfolds, blockchain's role in shaping the data landscape will undoubtedly continue to evolve, benefiting individuals and businesses alike.

Overview of Blockchain Applications

In recent years, blockchain technology has emerged as a revolutionary force that is transforming various industries and sectors. The applications of blockchain extend far beyond its initial use case as the underlying technology behind cryptocurrencies like Bitcoin. This subchapter will provide an overview of the diverse range of applications that blockchain has in store for us, showcasing its potential to reshape the future of data storage and sharing.

One of the most prominent applications of blockchain is in the realm of finance and banking. Blockchain technology offers the promise of secure, transparent, and efficient financial transactions. With the use of smart contracts, financial agreements can be executed automatically, eliminating the need for intermediaries and reducing costs. Additionally, blockchain-based digital identities can enhance Know Your Customer (KYC) processes and streamline customer onboarding.

Another promising area where blockchain is making significant strides is supply chain management. The immutable and transparent nature of blockchain ensures the traceability and authenticity of goods throughout the supply chain. This can help combat counterfeit products, reduce fraud, and enable more efficient logistics and inventory management. By providing consumers with access to reliable and real-time information about the origin and journey of products, blockchain empowers individuals to make informed purchasing decisions.

Blockchain is also revolutionizing the healthcare industry by enabling secure and interoperable sharing of patient data. With blockchain, patients have greater control over their medical records while ensuring privacy and security. This technology can improve the accuracy and accessibility of medical information, leading to more effective diagnoses and treatments. Blockchain-based systems can also facilitate the tracking and authentication of pharmaceuticals, mitigating the risks associated with counterfeit drugs.

Beyond finance, supply chain, and healthcare, blockchain is finding applications in various other sectors such as energy, real estate, voting systems, intellectual property rights management, and more. The potential of blockchain to transform these industries lies in its ability to create trust, enhance security, and enable decentralized, peer-to-peer interactions.

As more organizations and industries recognize the benefits and possibilities offered by blockchain, the technology continues to evolve and mature. However, it is important to note that blockchain is not a one-size-fits-all solution. Each application requires careful consideration of its unique requirements and challenges. Nonetheless, by exploring the potential of blockchain and understanding its capabilities, we can unlock a future where data storage and sharing are secure, transparent, and efficient across various domains.

In the subsequent chapters of this book, we will delve deeper into the specific applications of blockchain in different industries, examining the opportunities, challenges, and future prospects that lie ahead. Whether you are a blockchain enthusiast, a business leader, or simply curious about the technology, this book aims to provide you with a comprehensive understanding of blockchain's role in shaping the future of data storage and sharing.

Chapter 2: The Need for Secure Data Storage and Sharing

Importance of Data Security

In today's digital age, data has become the lifeblood of every industry and organization. From personal information to financial records, businesses rely on data to make informed decisions and provide valuable services to their customers. However, with the increasing reliance on digital platforms and interconnected systems, the risk of data breaches has also skyrocketed. This is where data security, especially in the realm of blockchain technology, plays a pivotal role.

Blockchain, a decentralized and immutable digital ledger, offers a unique solution to the data security conundrum. By utilizing cryptographic techniques, blockchain ensures that data is securely stored and shared without the need for a centralized authority. This decentralized nature makes it extremely difficult for hackers to tamper with or gain unauthorized access to the data.

The importance of data security, especially within the blockchain niche, cannot be overstated. With traditional centralized systems, data breaches have become alarmingly common, leading to severe consequences such as identity theft, financial fraud, and loss of trust among consumers. Blockchain technology, on the other hand, provides an unprecedented level of security, making it an ideal solution for industries dealing with sensitive data, such as healthcare, finance, and supply chain management.

One of the key features of blockchain technology is its ability to create an immutable record of transactions. Once a data entry is added to the blockchain, it becomes virtually impossible to alter or delete it without leaving a trace. This feature ensures data integrity and eliminates the risk of unauthorized modifications. Furthermore, the decentralized nature of blockchain means that there is no single point of failure, making it highly resistant to hacking attempts and ensuring data availability even in the face of cyberattacks.

Moreover, blockchain technology employs advanced cryptographic techniques to protect data during transmission and storage. Each transaction or data entry is encrypted and linked to the previous entry, forming a chain of blocks. This cryptographic security ensures that only authorized parties can access the data, while maintaining the privacy and confidentiality of sensitive information.

In conclusion, data security is of utmost importance in today's digital landscape, and blockchain technology provides a robust solution to address this concern. Its decentralized nature, immutability, and strong cryptographic techniques make it an ideal choice for industries that handle sensitive data. By embracing blockchain, organizations can not only safeguard their data but also build trust among their customers and stakeholders. As the future unfolds, the role of blockchain in secure storage and sharing of data will continue to be at the forefront of technological advancements.

Challenges and Risks in Traditional Data Storage and Sharing

In today's digital age, data has emerged as one of the most valuable assets for individuals, businesses, and organizations across the globe. However, traditional data storage and sharing methods have inherent challenges and risks that can compromise the integrity, security, and privacy of this valuable information. This subchapter explores these challenges and risks, highlighting the need for a more secure and efficient solution - blockchain technology.

One of the primary challenges with traditional data storage is the vulnerability to cyber attacks. Centralized storage systems, where data is stored in a single location, are susceptible to hacking and unauthorized access. High-profile data breaches, such as those experienced by major corporations and government entities, have exposed the weaknesses of these traditional methods. The risks associated with data breaches include identity theft, financial loss, and reputational damage.

Another challenge is the lack of transparency and trust in traditional data storage and sharing. Centralized systems often rely on intermediaries, such as cloud service providers or data storage companies, to manage and secure data. This reliance on third parties introduces a level of opacity, making it difficult to verify the integrity and authenticity of the stored data. Additionally, the sharing of data between different organizations or individuals can be cumbersome, requiring complex agreements and intermediaries.

Data privacy is another significant concern in traditional data storage. With centralized systems, individuals often have limited control over their personal data, which can be collected, analyzed, and sold by various entities without their consent. This lack of control over personal information raises ethical and legal issues, as well as potential misuse of data.

Blockchain technology offers a promising solution to address these challenges and risks. By leveraging decentralization, encryption, and consensus mechanisms, blockchain provides a secure and transparent platform for data storage and sharing. With blockchain, data is stored across a network of computers, making it highly resistant to hacking and unauthorized access. The tamper-proof nature of blockchain ensures the integrity and authenticity of the stored data, eliminating the need for intermediaries and enabling direct peer-to-peer data sharing.

Furthermore, blockchain technology enables individuals to have full control over their data through encryption and decentralized identity management. Users can determine who has access to their data and under what conditions, enhancing privacy and consent. The immutability of blockchain also ensures that data cannot be altered or deleted without consensus, providing a reliable source of truth.

In conclusion, traditional data storage and sharing methods pose significant challenges and risks in terms of security, transparency, and privacy. Blockchain technology offers a transformative solution to address these issues, providing a secure, transparent, and decentralized platform for data storage and sharing. By embracing blockchain, individuals, businesses, and organizations can mitigate the risks associated with traditional data storage, paving the way for a future where data is truly secure and controlled by its rightful owners.

Exploring Existing Solutions

In the fast-paced digital era we live in, data has become the new currency. From personal information to business records, the need for secure storage and sharing has never been more crucial. As the world evolves, so do the solutions available to address this pressing issue. In this subchapter, we will delve into the existing solutions that have emerged, with a particular focus on the revolutionary technology known as blockchain.

Blockchain, the underlying technology behind cryptocurrencies like Bitcoin, has gained immense popularity and recognition for its potential to revolutionize various industries. However, its impact on data storage and sharing is still being explored.

One existing solution that has gained traction is cloud storage. Cloud storage providers offer scalable and cost-effective solutions for storing and accessing data. However, concerns about data privacy and security have raised questions about the reliability of these solutions. Blockchain technology, with its decentralized and immutable nature, offers a potential solution to these concerns. By utilizing blockchain, data can be securely stored and accessed without relying on a single centralized entity, reducing the risk of data breaches and unauthorized access.

Another existing solution is the use of encryption techniques. Encryption ensures that data is transformed into a coded format that can only be deciphered with the right decryption key. While encryption provides a level of security, the centralized nature of the encryption systems still poses vulnerabilities. Blockchain technology can enhance encryption by decentralizing the storage and access to encryption keys, making it even more secure and resistant to attacks.

Furthermore, existing data sharing platforms, such as file-sharing services or collaborative platforms, often suffer from issues related to data integrity and trust. Blockchain technology could provide a solution by enabling transparent and tamper-proof records of data transactions, ensuring the integrity and authenticity of shared data.

While these existing solutions have made significant progress in data storage and sharing, the integration of blockchain technology holds the potential to revolutionize the way we secure and share data. Blockchain's decentralized nature, immutability, and transparency offer a promising foundation for enhancing existing solutions and addressing the challenges associated with data security and privacy.

In conclusion, exploring existing solutions is crucial to understanding the current landscape of data storage and sharing. Cloud storage, encryption techniques, and data sharing platforms have paved the way, but the integration of blockchain technology has the potential to take data security and sharing to a whole new level. The future of data is evolving, and blockchain is set to play a significant role in shaping a more secure and trustworthy digital world for EVERY ONE involved in the blockchain niche.

Introducing Blockchain as a Secure Alternative

In recent years, the world has witnessed a rapid transformation in the way data is stored and shared. Traditional centralized systems have become increasingly vulnerable to cyber threats, data breaches, and unauthorized access. As a result, the need for a more secure and transparent solution has emerged. Enter blockchain technology, a revolutionary innovation that has the potential to reshape the future of data storage and sharing.

Blockchain, at its core, is a decentralized digital ledger that records transactions across multiple computers. Unlike traditional systems where data is stored in a single location, blockchain distributes information across a network of computers, making it virtually impossible for a single point of failure or malicious attack. This decentralized nature ensures that data remains secure and tamper-proof, creating a new level of trust and transparency.

One of the key features that make blockchain a secure alternative is its immutability. Once data is added to a blockchain, it becomes virtually impossible to alter or delete it. This feature eliminates the risk of unauthorized modifications, ensuring the integrity and authenticity of the stored information. Whether it's financial transactions, medical records, or supply chain data, blockchain provides a robust solution that protects sensitive information from tampering.

Furthermore, blockchain's secure and transparent nature significantly reduces the risk of data breaches. In traditional systems, a single breach can compromise vast amounts of data. With blockchain, each transaction is encrypted and linked to the previous one, creating an unbroken chain of secure information. This makes it incredibly difficult for hackers to access or manipulate data, as any unauthorized changes would be instantly detected and rejected by the network.

The potential applications of blockchain extend far beyond financial transactions. Industries such as healthcare, supply chain management, and even voting systems can greatly benefit from this secure alternative. Imagine a world where patients have complete control over their medical records, supply chains are fully traceable from start to finish, and elections are free from fraud or manipulation. Blockchain has the power to revolutionize these sectors, ensuring data integrity, privacy, and security for all.

In conclusion, blockchain technology holds immense promise for the future of data storage and sharing. Its secure and decentralized nature provides a much-needed alternative to traditional systems that are susceptible to cyber threats. From financial transactions to healthcare records, blockchain has the potential to revolutionize various industries, offering a level of security, transparency, and trust that was previously unimaginable. As we embrace this technology, we pave the way for a future where data is protected, and individuals have full control over their information.

Chapter 3: Fundamentals of Data Storage and Sharing on Blockchain

Decentralization and Immutability in Blockchain

Blockchain technology has revolutionized the way we store and share data, providing a secure and transparent system that has the potential to transform industries across the globe. At the heart of this technology are two key principles: decentralization and immutability.

Decentralization is a core feature of blockchain that sets it apart from traditional centralized systems. In a decentralized network, there is no single point of control or authority. Instead, the power is distributed among multiple participants, known as nodes, who collectively maintain the integrity of the blockchain. This distributed nature of blockchain ensures that no single entity can manipulate or alter the data stored within the system.

The benefits of decentralization are manifold. First and foremost, it enhances the security of the network. Since there is no central authority, hackers would need to compromise a majority of the nodes to tamper with the data, making it highly resistant to attacks. Additionally, decentralization eliminates the need for intermediaries, such as banks or government agencies, reducing costs and increasing efficiency in various processes, including financial transactions, supply chain management, and identity verification.

Immutability, on the other hand, refers to the inability to change or alter the data once it has been recorded on the blockchain. Every transaction or piece of information is stored in a block, which is linked to the previous block through a cryptographic hash function. This link ensures that any changes made to a block would require the modification of all subsequent blocks, making it nearly impossible to tamper with the data without the consensus of the network.

The immutability of blockchain ensures transparency and trust in the system. It allows participants to verify the authenticity and integrity of the data, eliminating the need for third-party audits or intermediaries. This feature has immense implications for industries that heavily rely on trust and accountability, such as finance, healthcare, and supply chain management.

In conclusion, decentralization and immutability are two fundamental principles that underpin the power and potential of blockchain technology. By distributing control and ensuring the integrity of data, blockchain offers a secure and transparent system that can revolutionize various industries. As we move towards a future driven by data, understanding these principles becomes crucial for individuals and businesses alike, as they navigate the transformative role of blockchain in secure storage and sharing.

Data Encryption and Privacy on Blockchain

In today's digital age, data has become one of the most valuable assets. From personal information to financial records, the amount of data generated and stored is astronomical. However, with the increasing prevalence of cyber threats and privacy concerns, it is crucial to find secure and reliable methods of storing and sharing this data. This is where blockchain technology comes into play.

Blockchain, the technology behind cryptocurrencies like Bitcoin, is a decentralized and immutable ledger that offers unprecedented security and transparency. By leveraging its unique features, such as immutability and cryptography, blockchain provides an ideal solution for data encryption and privacy.

One of the key advantages of blockchain technology is its ability to encrypt data. When data is stored on a blockchain, it is encrypted using advanced cryptographic algorithms. This means that the data is converted into unreadable code, which can only be deciphered by authorized parties with the correct decryption key. This ensures that even if the data is intercepted or accessed by unauthorized individuals, it remains secure and confidential.

Moreover, blockchain offers enhanced privacy features through its decentralized nature. Unlike traditional centralized systems, where data is stored in a single location and controlled by a central authority, blockchain stores data across a network of computers called nodes. Each node has a copy of the entire blockchain, and every transaction is verified and recorded by multiple nodes. This decentralized architecture eliminates the need for a central authority, reducing the risk of data breaches and unauthorized access.

In addition to encryption and decentralization, blockchain also provides transparency and accountability. Every transaction recorded on the blockchain is time-stamped and linked to previous transactions, creating an unalterable chain of information. This transparency ensures that all data exchanges are traceable and auditable, making it easier to identify any potential security breaches or unauthorized activities.

By embracing blockchain technology, individuals and organizations can significantly enhance their data encryption and privacy. Whether it is personal data, financial records, or sensitive business information, blockchain provides a secure and immutable platform for storing and sharing data. It empowers users to have control over their data and decide who can access it, mitigating the risks associated with centralized data storage.

In conclusion, data encryption and privacy are paramount in today's digital world. Blockchain technology offers a promising solution to address these concerns. Its encryption capabilities, decentralized architecture, and transparency make it an ideal choice for secure data storage and sharing. As blockchain continues to evolve, it is expected to revolutionize the way data is managed, ensuring a future where privacy and security are at the forefront of digital interactions.

Smart Contracts for Data Storage and Sharing

In recent years, blockchain technology has gained significant attention for its potential to revolutionize various industries. One area where blockchain shows immense promise is in the field of data storage and sharing. With the rise of smart contracts, blockchain offers a secure and transparent solution for managing and exchanging data. This subchapter explores the concept of smart contracts for data storage and sharing, highlighting their benefits and potential applications.

Smart contracts, essentially self-executing contracts with the terms of the agreement directly written into code, provide a decentralized and tamper-proof method for automating processes. When applied to data storage and sharing, smart contracts eliminate the need for intermediaries, such as cloud storage providers or centralized platforms, reducing costs and enhancing security. By leveraging the immutability and transparency of blockchain, smart contracts ensure that data is securely stored, verified, and shared.

One of the key advantages of using smart contracts for data storage and sharing is enhanced security. Traditional data storage systems are vulnerable to hacking and data breaches due to their centralized nature. However, with blockchain and smart contracts, data is encrypted, fragmented, and distributed across a network of nodes. This decentralized approach ensures that even if one node is compromised, the data remains secure due to the consensus mechanism of blockchain.

Furthermore, smart contracts enable individuals and organizations to have full control and ownership of their data. By eliminating the need for third-party intermediaries, individuals can securely store and share their data without relying on centralized platforms. This empowers users to decide who can access their data and under what conditions, enhancing privacy and data sovereignty.

The applications of smart contracts for data storage and sharing are vast. For instance, in the healthcare industry, sensitive patient data can be securely stored on the blockchain, allowing authorized healthcare providers to access and update the information while ensuring patient privacy. Similarly, in supply chain management, smart contracts can facilitate transparent and efficient tracking of products, reducing fraud and counterfeiting.

In conclusion, smart contracts offer a revolutionary approach to data storage and sharing by leveraging the security and transparency of blockchain technology. By eliminating intermediaries and enhancing security, smart contracts empower individuals and organizations to securely store, verify, and share their data. The potential applications of smart contracts for data storage and sharing are limitless, promising a future where individuals have full control and ownership of their data while enjoying enhanced privacy and security. Embracing this technology has the potential to reshape industries and unlock new possibilities in the world of data.

Consensus Mechanisms for Data Integrity

In the world of blockchain technology, consensus mechanisms play a crucial role in ensuring the integrity and security of data. These mechanisms form the backbone of decentralized networks, allowing participants to agree on the state of a shared ledger and validate transactions without the need for a central authority.

Consensus mechanisms are essential for maintaining the trust and transparency that blockchain technology offers. They enable different nodes in a network to reach an agreement on the validity of data and prevent malicious actors from tampering or manipulating information stored on the blockchain.

One of the most well-known consensus mechanisms is Proof of Work (PoW), which is used by popular cryptocurrencies like Bitcoin. PoW requires network participants, known as miners, to solve complex mathematical puzzles to validate transactions and add them to the blockchain. This mechanism ensures that a significant amount of computational power is expended, making it difficult for any single entity to control the network.

Another consensus mechanism gaining traction is Proof of Stake (PoS). PoS eliminates the need for miners and instead relies on participants, known as validators, to hold and lock up a certain amount of cryptocurrency as a stake in the network. Validators are then chosen to validate transactions based on their stake, with higher stakes resulting in a greater chance of being selected. This mechanism reduces the energy consumption associated with PoW and encourages participants to act in the best interest of the network.

Other consensus mechanisms, such as Delegated Proof of Stake (DPoS), Practical Byzantine Fault Tolerance (PBFT), and Proof of Authority (PoA), offer different approaches to achieving consensus while prioritizing factors such as scalability, speed, and fault tolerance.

Understanding the various consensus mechanisms is essential for anyone involved in the blockchain ecosystem. Whether you are a developer, investor, or simply curious about the technology, having knowledge of consensus mechanisms can help you make informed decisions and navigate the rapidly evolving landscape of blockchain.

Consensus mechanisms are not limited to cryptocurrencies; they have the potential to revolutionize various industries, including supply chain management, healthcare, finance, and more. By leveraging blockchain and consensus mechanisms, organizations can establish trust, enhance security, and streamline processes by eliminating the need for intermediaries and central authorities.

In conclusion, consensus mechanisms are the foundation of secure and trustworthy blockchain networks. They ensure data integrity by enabling participants to agree on the validity of transactions and prevent tampering. As blockchain technology continues to evolve and find applications in diverse industries, understanding the different consensus mechanisms becomes increasingly important for anyone interested in the potential of blockchain.

Chapter 4: Use Cases of Blockchain in Secure Data Storage

Healthcare Industry

The healthcare industry is one of the most critical sectors worldwide, affecting every individual regardless of age, gender, or social status. It plays a pivotal role in preserving and improving the overall well-being of communities. However, despite its significance, the healthcare industry faces numerous challenges such as data security, interoperability, and patient privacy. In this subchapter, we will explore how blockchain technology can revolutionize the healthcare industry and address these pressing issues.

Blockchain, the underlying technology behind cryptocurrencies like Bitcoin, has gained significant attention in recent years due to its potential to transform various sectors. This decentralized and distributed ledger system offers a transparent and secure way to store, manage, and share data. By leveraging blockchain, the healthcare industry can overcome several obstacles it currently faces.

One of the most significant challenges in the healthcare industry is the security of sensitive patient data. Traditional centralized databases are vulnerable to cyberattacks and data breaches. However, blockchain's cryptographic algorithms and consensus mechanisms make it highly secure. It enables healthcare organizations to store patient records on the blockchain, ensuring that they are tamper-proof and protected from unauthorized access.

Moreover, blockchain can enhance data interoperability, which refers to the ability of different healthcare systems to exchange and make use of data seamlessly. Currently, healthcare providers often struggle with incompatible systems and fragmented data, hindering effective collaboration and patient care. By implementing blockchain-based solutions, healthcare organizations can create a unified and standardized platform for sharing medical records, improving care coordination, and reducing medical errors.

In addition to security and interoperability, blockchain also addresses patient privacy concerns. With blockchain, individuals have control over their health data, allowing them to grant access to healthcare providers on a need-to-know basis. This empowers patients to maintain ownership of their personal information, giving them confidence and control over how their data is used.

Blockchain technology has the potential to revolutionize the healthcare industry, transforming how data is stored, shared, and utilized. By leveraging blockchain, healthcare organizations can enhance data security, improve interoperability, and protect patient privacy. These advancements will ultimately result in more efficient healthcare systems, better patient outcomes, and a higher level of trust in the industry.

In conclusion, blockchain's role in the healthcare industry is promising. This subchapter has provided an overview of how blockchain technology can address the challenges faced by the healthcare industry, including data security, interoperability, and patient privacy. As the world continues to embrace digital transformation, blockchain is poised to play a crucial role in shaping the future of healthcare.

Financial Services Sector

The financial services sector plays a crucial role in the global economy, providing a wide range of services that facilitate economic growth and development. In recent years, this sector has witnessed significant disruptions and transformations, largely driven by the emergence of blockchain technology. This subchapter aims to explore the impact of blockchain on the financial services sector and the potential it holds for secure storage and sharing of data.

Blockchain technology, at its core, is a decentralized and immutable digital ledger that enables secure and transparent transactions. Its inherent characteristics make it an ideal solution for the financial services industry, which heavily relies on trust, security, and accuracy of data. Blockchain eliminates the need for intermediaries, reduces transaction costs, and enhances the efficiency and speed of financial transactions.

One of the key areas where blockchain is revolutionizing the financial services sector is in cross-border payments and remittances. Traditional methods of transferring money across borders are often slow, expensive, and subject to high fees. Blockchain-based solutions enable near-instantaneous, low-cost, and secure transactions, benefiting both individuals and businesses.

Furthermore, blockchain has the potential to transform the way we think about identity verification and access to financial services. With blockchain, individuals can have full control over their personal data, securely storing it on the blockchain and selectively sharing it with trusted parties. This eliminates the need for multiple identity verification processes and reduces the risk of identity theft and fraud.

The use of smart contracts, another application of blockchain technology, has the potential to streamline and automate various financial services processes. Smart contracts are self-executing contracts with the terms of the agreement directly written into lines of code. They eliminate the need for intermediaries, reduce costs, and enhance the speed and accuracy of transactions.

While blockchain holds immense potential for the financial services sector, it also presents challenges and considerations. Scalability, privacy, regulatory compliance, and interoperability are among the key issues that need to be addressed to fully realize the benefits of blockchain in the financial services sector.

In conclusion, blockchain technology is reshaping the financial services sector, providing secure storage and sharing of data, enhancing transaction speed and efficiency, and revolutionizing traditional processes. Its potential to transform cross-border payments, identity verification, and smart contracts is immense. However, it is crucial to address the challenges associated with blockchain adoption to fully harness its benefits in the financial services sector.

Supply Chain Management

In today's globalized world, where goods and services are sourced and delivered from various corners of the world, efficient supply chain management has become paramount. It ensures that products reach the end consumers in a timely, cost-effective, and sustainable manner. However, traditional supply chain processes are often plagued with inefficiencies, lack of transparency, and trust issues.

This subchapter explores the potential of blockchain technology in revolutionizing supply chain management. Blockchain, the underlying technology behind cryptocurrencies like Bitcoin, offers a decentralized and secure way of recording, verifying, and tracking transactions. Its distributed ledger system enables real-time visibility, transparency, and immutability, making it an ideal solution for supply chain management.

First and foremost, blockchain can address the lack of transparency and trust within supply chains. With a blockchain-based system, all participants, from suppliers to manufacturers to retailers, can have real-time access to a shared ledger. This allows for complete visibility into the movement and origin of goods, reducing the risk of fraud, counterfeit products, and unethical practices. Moreover, since blockchain records are immutable, any tampering or alteration of data is nearly impossible, ensuring the integrity of the supply chain.

Furthermore, blockchain can streamline supply chain processes by automating and optimizing workflows. Smart contracts, self-executing agreements stored on the blockchain, can automate tasks such as order fulfillment, payment processing, and inventory management. This not only reduces the time and effort required for manual coordination but also minimizes errors and delays. Additionally, by eliminating intermediaries and reducing paperwork, blockchain can significantly reduce costs associated with supply chain operations.

Another critical aspect of supply chain management is ensuring sustainability and ethical sourcing. Blockchain can enable the tracking of every stage of a product's journey, from raw material extraction to manufacturing to distribution. This enables companies and consumers to verify the authenticity, quality, and sustainability of products, promoting responsible sourcing and environmentally friendly practices.

In conclusion, blockchain technology has the potential to revolutionize supply chain management by providing transparency, trust, and efficiency. As companies strive to meet the demands of an increasingly globalized and conscious consumer base, implementing blockchain-based solutions can help ensure the integrity, sustainability, and cost-effectiveness of their supply chains. By embracing this transformative technology, businesses can unlock new opportunities for growth, while consumers can make more informed and ethical purchasing decisions.

Government and Public Records

In this subchapter, we will delve into the crucial role that blockchain technology can play in the management of government and public records. Traditionally, these records have been stored in centralized databases, making them vulnerable to hacking, data breaches, and tampering. Blockchain, with its decentralized and immutable nature, provides a secure and transparent solution for the storage and sharing of these records.

Government agencies are responsible for maintaining a vast array of records, ranging from birth and death certificates to land titles and property deeds. These records are not only critical for administrative purposes but also for ensuring the integrity of our legal and regulatory systems. Unfortunately, the current systems are often plagued by inefficiency, bureaucracy, and the risk of fraud.

By leveraging blockchain technology, governments can create a decentralized and tamper-proof repository for public records. Each record can be securely stored on the blockchain, with its authenticity and integrity verified by consensus mechanisms. This eliminates the need for intermediaries and reduces the risk of corruption or unauthorized modification.

Furthermore, blockchain can enhance the accessibility and transparency of public records. Instead of relying on physical visits or time-consuming paperwork, individuals can access their records digitally through a secure blockchain network. This streamlines processes, saves time, and reduces administrative costs.

Another significant advantage of blockchain technology is its ability to facilitate secure and auditable transactions. For instance, when it comes to property transactions, blockchain can ensure that the ownership history is transparent and verifiable. This reduces the risk of fraud and enhances trust between buyers, sellers, and financial institutions.

Moreover, blockchain-based public records can also empower citizens by giving them more control over their personal data. With blockchain, individuals can grant access to specific records or attributes on a need-to-know basis, ensuring privacy while still enabling necessary information sharing.

In conclusion, blockchain technology holds immense potential in revolutionizing the management of government and public records. By eliminating intermediaries, enhancing transparency, and providing a secure and auditable platform, blockchain can significantly improve the efficiency, security, and trustworthiness of public record systems. Its decentralized nature ensures that records are not subject to a single point of failure, making it an ideal solution for ensuring the integrity and accessibility of government and public records.

Education and Credential Verification

In today's digital age, the importance of education and credentials cannot be overstated. Whether you are a student looking to enter the workforce, an employer seeking qualified candidates, or a professional looking to enhance your career prospects, reliable and secure verification of education and credentials is crucial. This subchapter explores how blockchain technology is revolutionizing the way we verify and share educational achievements.

Blockchain, the underlying technology behind cryptocurrencies like Bitcoin, has gained significant attention in recent years for its potential to transform various industries. One such industry that stands to benefit greatly from blockchain is education. With the decentralized and immutable nature of blockchain, educational institutions can now securely store and share student records and achievements, eliminating the need for traditional paper-based transcripts and certificates.

One of the key advantages of using blockchain for education and credential verification is the enhanced transparency it provides. Blockchain allows for a decentralized ledger that can be accessed by multiple parties, ensuring that the information is accurate and tamper-proof. This transparency helps prevent fraud and ensures that only legitimate credentials are recognized.

Moreover, blockchain eliminates the need for intermediaries in the verification process. Instead of relying on third-party verification services, employers can directly access the blockchain to verify a candidate's educational background, saving time and reducing costs.

This streamlined process also minimizes the risk of human error and ensures that individuals are recognized for their true qualifications.

Another significant benefit of blockchain-based education verification is the potential for lifelong learning and skill tracking. As individuals pursue continuous education and acquire new skills throughout their careers, blockchain can serve as a reliable and comprehensive record of their achievements. This allows for a more accurate representation of an individual's knowledge and expertise, making it easier for employers to identify the right candidate for a particular job.

In conclusion, blockchain technology has the potential to revolutionize education and credential verification. Its transparency, security, and efficiency make it an ideal solution for ensuring the accuracy and reliability of educational records. By embracing blockchain, educational institutions, employers, and individuals can benefit from a more streamlined and trustworthy verification process. The future of education and credential verification lies in the power of blockchain.

Chapter 5: The Future of Data Storage and Sharing with Blockchain

Evolving Trends and Innovations in Blockchain Technology

Blockchain technology has come a long way since its inception with the introduction of Bitcoin. It has emerged as a revolutionary force, disrupting industries and transforming the way we store and share data securely. As we move forward, the future of blockchain holds exciting possibilities, with several evolving trends and innovations set to shape its trajectory.

One of the most notable trends in blockchain technology is the rise of smart contracts. These self-executing contracts eliminate the need for intermediaries and enable the automation of processes in a transparent and secure manner. Smart contracts have the potential to revolutionize various industries, including finance, supply chain management, and real estate. They offer increased efficiency, reduced costs, and enhanced trust, making them an attractive proposition for businesses and individuals alike.

Another significant trend is the emergence of blockchain interoperability. As the number of blockchain networks grows, the ability to communicate and share data seamlessly between different platforms becomes crucial. Interoperability allows for the integration of multiple blockchains, enabling cross-chain transactions and fostering collaboration between different networks. This trend holds immense potential for enhancing scalability, connectivity, and overall utility of blockchain technology.

Furthermore, the concept of decentralized finance (DeFi) has gained significant traction in recent years. DeFi refers to the use of blockchain technology to recreate traditional financial systems in a decentralized manner. It enables individuals to access financial services such as lending, borrowing, and investing without the need for intermediaries or centralized authorities. DeFi has the potential to democratize finance, providing equal opportunities to individuals worldwide, regardless of their background or location.

In terms of innovation, blockchain technology is witnessing advancements in areas such as privacy and scalability. Privacy-focused blockchains are being developed to address concerns surrounding data privacy and confidentiality. These solutions utilize cryptographic techniques to ensure the secure and anonymous transfer of data, making them ideal for applications such as healthcare, identity management, and voting systems.

Scalability remains a key challenge for blockchain technology, especially as it gains mainstream adoption. However, innovative solutions such as sharding, layer-two protocols, and off-chain transactions are being explored to improve the scalability of blockchain networks. These advancements aim to increase transaction throughput, reduce fees, and enhance the overall user experience.

In conclusion, blockchain technology continues to evolve, bringing forth exciting trends and innovations. From the rise of smart contracts and interoperability to the emergence of DeFi and advancements in privacy and scalability, the future of blockchain holds immense potential. As blockchain technology becomes more accessible and integrated into various industries, it is essential for everyone, regardless of their niche, to stay informed and embrace the opportunities it presents.

Potential Challenges and Scalability Issues

In the rapidly evolving world of data storage and sharing, blockchain technology has emerged as a promising solution. With its decentralized and secure nature, it offers a new way of managing and protecting sensitive information. However, like any emerging technology, blockchain faces its fair share of challenges and scalability issues that need to be addressed.

One of the major challenges faced by blockchain is scalability. As more users join the network and the volume of data being stored and shared increases, the blockchain can become slow and inefficient. This is primarily due to the consensus mechanism employed by most blockchains, such as proof-of-work, which requires time-consuming computations to validate transactions. As a result, the network can experience delays and bottlenecks, hindering its ability to handle a large number of transactions simultaneously.

Another challenge is the energy consumption associated with blockchain technology. As mentioned earlier, proof-of-work requires extensive computational power, resulting in high energy consumption. This not only contributes to environmental concerns but also limits the scalability of the technology. As the blockchain network grows, the energy required to sustain it becomes a significant challenge that needs to be addressed.

Furthermore, interoperability between different blockchains is a crucial challenge for the future of data storage and sharing. Currently, there are numerous blockchain platforms, each with its own unique features and protocols. However, these different blockchains often operate in isolation, hindering the seamless transfer and sharing of data between them. Achieving interoperability would require the development of standardized protocols and frameworks, allowing efficient communication and data exchange between different blockchain networks.

Security is another concern when it comes to blockchain technology. While the underlying technology is inherently secure, the applications built on top of it may still have vulnerabilities. Smart contracts, for example, can be susceptible to bugs or malicious attacks, compromising the integrity and security of the stored data. As blockchain continues to evolve, it is essential to invest in robust security measures and conduct regular audits to mitigate any potential risks.

In conclusion, while blockchain technology holds immense potential for secure data storage and sharing, it also faces several challenges and scalability issues. Addressing these challenges, such as scalability, energy consumption, interoperability, and security, is crucial for the widespread adoption and success of blockchain technology. By investing in research, innovation, and collaboration, we can overcome these obstacles and pave the way for a future where blockchain plays a central role in the way we store and share data securely.

Regulation and Legal Implications

In the rapidly evolving world of blockchain technology, it is crucial to understand the regulatory and legal implications that govern its use. As blockchain continues to disrupt industries and reshape the way we store and share data, it is important for everyone, including blockchain enthusiasts, businesses, and policymakers, to be aware of the legal framework surrounding this transformative technology.

One of the key aspects that regulators and lawmakers are grappling with is the classification of cryptocurrencies and tokens that are built on blockchain networks. Are they considered securities, commodities, or something entirely new? This determination has significant consequences for entities issuing tokens and individuals trading or investing in them. It impacts the level of regulation they are subject to, including securities laws, anti-money laundering regulations, and tax obligations.

Furthermore, the use of blockchain in storing and sharing data raises questions about data privacy and protection. As blockchain is inherently transparent and immutable, concerns arise regarding the exposure of personal or sensitive information. Striking a balance between the benefits of transparency and the need for data protection becomes a critical challenge for regulators.

Additionally, the global nature of blockchain technology brings forth jurisdictional issues. With transactions occurring across borders and decentralized networks, it becomes essential to establish a harmonized legal framework that accommodates cross-border blockchain transactions and disputes. Collaborative efforts among countries are necessary to ensure consistent regulations and avoid regulatory arbitrage.

Intellectual property rights and licensing are also areas of legal consideration. As blockchain enables the creation of decentralized applications (DApps) and smart contracts, the ownership and licensing of these innovations become crucial. Intellectual property laws need to evolve to address the unique challenges posed by blockchain technology, ensuring that innovators are rewarded and protected for their contributions.

In conclusion, as blockchain technology gains wider adoption and disrupts various industries, understanding the regulatory and legal implications becomes paramount for everyone involved. Policymakers must strike a delicate balance between fostering innovation and protecting consumers and investors. Businesses need to navigate the evolving legal landscape to ensure compliance and mitigate risks. Individuals must be aware of their rights and responsibilities when engaging with blockchain technology. By addressing these challenges and working towards a comprehensive and globally harmonized legal framework, we can unlock the full potential of blockchain technology while safeguarding the interests of all stakeholders.

Collaboration and Interoperability among Blockchain Networks

In the fast-paced digital era, blockchain technology has emerged as a groundbreaking solution for secure storage and sharing of data. As its potential continues to be unlocked, it's crucial to explore the concept of collaboration and interoperability among blockchain networks. This subchapter aims to delve into the significance of these aspects, addressing not only the blockchain community but also a wider audience interested in the future of data.

Blockchain, at its core, is a decentralized ledger that allows multiple participants to maintain a shared and immutable record of transactions. However, the true power of blockchain lies in its ability to foster collaboration among various networks. By enabling different blockchains to communicate and interact seamlessly, we can create a global ecosystem that transcends individual networks' limitations.

Interoperability is the key to unlocking this potential. It refers to the ability of different blockchain networks to understand, communicate, and transact with one another. Achieving interoperability requires the development of standardized protocols and interfaces that facilitate seamless data transfer and transaction execution. Such interoperability would enable users to leverage the advantages of multiple blockchain networks simultaneously, resulting in enhanced efficiency, scalability, and innovation.

Collaboration among blockchain networks also opens up new opportunities for businesses and individuals. It allows for the creation of cross-chain applications, where data and assets can be securely exchanged across multiple networks. For instance, a supply chain management application could seamlessly integrate data from various blockchains, ensuring transparency and traceability throughout the entire process. This collaborative approach eliminates silos, reduces redundancies, and fosters synergy among blockchain ecosystems.

Moreover, collaboration and interoperability are essential for achieving mass adoption of blockchain technology. With the ability to interconnect different networks, blockchain becomes more accessible to a wider range of users, regardless of their preferred platform or network. This inclusivity strengthens the overall blockchain community and propels the technology's growth.

As the blockchain landscape evolves, addressing the challenges associated with collaboration and interoperability becomes paramount. Developing standardized protocols, creating open-source frameworks, and establishing cross-chain communication channels are some of the steps towards achieving a harmonious and interconnected blockchain ecosystem.

In conclusion, collaboration and interoperability among blockchain networks hold immense potential for revolutionizing the future of data storage and sharing. By enabling seamless communication and interaction between different networks, we can unlock unprecedented levels of efficiency, scalability, and innovation. This subchapter aims to shed light on the significance of this aspect, appealing not only to the blockchain community but also to a broader audience interested in the transformative power of blockchain technology.

Chapter 6: Implementing Blockchain for Secure Data Storage and Sharing

Assessing Organizational Readiness

In today's digital age, the importance of data security and efficient sharing has become paramount. As organizations strive to stay ahead of the curve, they are increasingly turning to emerging technologies like blockchain to address their data storage and sharing needs. However, before implementing blockchain solutions, it is crucial for organizations to assess their readiness to embrace this transformative technology.

Assessing organizational readiness involves evaluating various aspects such as technical infrastructure, human resources, and cultural mindset. It requires a comprehensive analysis to determine whether an organization possesses the necessary capabilities and resources to successfully adopt and integrate blockchain into its existing systems.

One of the key factors to assess is the organization's technical infrastructure. Is the existing infrastructure capable of supporting blockchain technology? Are there any gaps that need to be addressed? Understanding the compatibility and scalability of the infrastructure is vital in determining the feasibility of blockchain adoption.

Another crucial aspect is the organization's human resources. Does the organization have the necessary expertise to implement and manage blockchain solutions? If not, is there a willingness to invest in training and upskilling employees? Blockchain technology requires specialized knowledge and skills, and organizations need to ensure they have the right personnel in place or the means to acquire them.

Furthermore, assessing the cultural mindset within the organization is equally important. Blockchain adoption often requires a shift in mindset and a willingness to embrace decentralized and transparent systems. It is essential to gauge whether the organization is open to change and willing to adapt its processes to accommodate the decentralized nature of blockchain technology.

Additionally, organizations must consider factors such as regulatory compliance and legal requirements. Blockchain technology operates within a specific legal and regulatory framework, and organizations need to assess whether their operations align with these requirements. Failure to comply with regulations can have severe consequences, and organizations must ensure they are prepared to navigate this complex landscape.

In conclusion, assessing organizational readiness is a critical step before implementing blockchain solutions. By evaluating technical infrastructure, human resources, cultural mindset, and regulatory compliance, organizations can determine their readiness to embrace this transformative technology. Taking the time to assess readiness will not only increase the chances of successful implementation but also pave the way for a more secure and efficient future of data storage and sharing.

Selecting the Right Blockchain Platform

In the rapidly evolving world of blockchain technology, it is crucial to choose the right platform that aligns with your specific needs and goals. With a plethora of blockchain platforms available, each offering unique features and capabilities, making an informed decision is of utmost importance. This chapter aims to guide you through the process of selecting the right blockchain platform that suits your requirements, whether you are an individual, a business, or a developer.

Understanding your needs is the first step towards finding the perfect blockchain platform. Consider the purpose for which you intend to use blockchain technology. Are you looking for a platform to create decentralized applications (dApps), conduct financial transactions, or establish a secure and transparent supply chain? Identifying your specific use case will help narrow down the options and select a platform that offers the necessary functionalities.

Next, evaluate the scalability and performance of the blockchain platform. As blockchain technology gains widespread adoption, it is essential to ensure that the platform you choose can handle a large volume of transactions without compromising speed or security. Look for platforms that offer high throughput and low latency, enabling seamless integration with existing systems and applications.

Security is another critical factor to consider when selecting a blockchain platform. Look for platforms that incorporate robust encryption mechanisms, decentralized consensus algorithms, and smart contract functionality to ensure the integrity and immutability of your data. Additionally, platforms that offer advanced security features like multi-factor authentication and permissioned access control should be given preference, especially for enterprise-level use cases.

Interoperability is an emerging aspect of blockchain technology that cannot be overlooked. As various blockchain platforms emerge, it is crucial to select a platform that can seamlessly communicate and share data with other platforms. Interoperability enables the exchange of assets, information, and services across different blockchain networks, fostering collaboration and expanding the possibilities of blockchain technology.

Finally, consider the community and ecosystem surrounding the blockchain platform. A thriving and supportive community ensures continuous development, updates, and adoption of the platform. Look for platforms with an active community, well-documented resources, and a range of development tools and libraries to facilitate rapid application development.

In conclusion, selecting the right blockchain platform requires a comprehensive understanding of your needs, scalability, security, interoperability, and community support. By conducting thorough research and evaluation, you can make an informed decision that aligns with your goals and maximizes the potential of blockchain technology.

Designing and Developing Blockchain Solutions

In today's digital age, where data security and privacy have become paramount concerns, blockchain technology has emerged as a game-changer. Blockchain, the underlying technology behind cryptocurrencies like Bitcoin, has revolutionized the way we store and share data securely. Its decentralized, transparent, and immutable nature makes it an ideal solution for a wide range of industries and applications.

This subchapter explores the intricacies of designing and developing blockchain solutions, providing insights into how this revolutionary technology can be harnessed to address the data challenges faced by businesses and individuals alike.

To begin with, understanding the fundamental concepts behind blockchain is crucial. We delve into the basics, explaining how blocks are created, linked together, and secured using advanced cryptographic algorithms. This knowledge lays the foundation for comprehending the design principles necessary for developing efficient and reliable blockchain solutions.

Next, we explore the various types of blockchain networks, such as public, private, and consortium blockchains, along with their respective use cases. We provide real-world examples, showcasing how organizations across industries have leveraged blockchain to streamline processes, enhance transparency, and improve security.

The chapter also delves into the intricacies of smart contracts, which are self-executing contracts with predefined rules encoded in the blockchain. We discuss how smart contracts can automate business processes, eliminate intermediaries, and ensure trust among parties, thereby revolutionizing traditional contractual agreements.

Furthermore, we address the challenges and considerations involved in designing and developing blockchain solutions. Scalability, interoperability, and energy consumption are among the crucial factors that need to be taken into account to ensure the successful implementation of blockchain technology.

Lastly, we provide guidance on how to start designing and developing blockchain solutions. From selecting the appropriate blockchain platform to designing the architecture and selecting consensus mechanisms, we outline the key steps and best practices to ensure a successful deployment.

With its potential to revolutionize data storage and sharing, blockchain technology has garnered significant attention across industries. This subchapter aims to empower readers with the necessary knowledge and insights to embark on their own blockchain journey. Whether you are a business owner, developer, or simply curious about the transformative power of blockchain, this subchapter will equip you with the understanding and tools to explore the possibilities of this groundbreaking technology.

Integration with Existing Systems

In the rapidly evolving world of technology, integration is key. As blockchain emerges as a groundbreaking solution for secure storage and sharing of data, it becomes essential to explore how it can seamlessly integrate with existing systems. This subchapter delves into the various aspects of integrating blockchain into different industries and the potential benefits it offers to organizations of all sizes.

Integration with existing systems is a critical consideration for any organization looking to adopt blockchain technology. Whether it is a financial institution, a supply chain management company, a healthcare provider, or a government agency, incorporating blockchain requires a thoughtful approach to ensure a smooth transition.

One of the primary advantages of integrating blockchain with existing systems is enhanced security. Blockchain's decentralized and immutable nature makes it highly resistant to tampering and fraud. By integrating blockchain, organizations can fortify their data storage and sharing processes, mitigating the risks associated with centralized systems. This is particularly relevant in industries that handle sensitive information, such as healthcare, finance, and identity verification.

Furthermore, integrating blockchain can lead to increased efficiency and transparency. The distributed ledger technology eliminates the need for intermediaries, streamlining processes and reducing costs. Smart contracts, a feature of blockchain, enable automated and self-executing agreements, eliminating the need for manual intervention.

This not only saves time but also ensures accuracy and reduces the chances of errors or disputes.

Integrating blockchain can also enable seamless collaboration between different entities and systems. With blockchain's decentralized architecture, organizations can securely share data and collaborate with partners, suppliers, and customers. This fosters trust, improves traceability, and enhances overall operational efficiency.

However, it is important to note that integrating blockchain with existing systems requires careful planning and consideration. Organizations must assess their specific needs and evaluate the compatibility of their current infrastructure with blockchain technology. They should also consider the scalability and interoperability of the chosen blockchain platform to ensure a sustainable integration.

In conclusion, integrating blockchain with existing systems holds immense potential for organizations across various industries. By leveraging blockchain's security, efficiency, transparency, and collaboration capabilities, businesses can revolutionize their data storage and sharing practices. As the technology continues to mature, it is vital for organizations to explore the possibilities of integrating blockchain, keeping in mind the unique requirements and challenges of their respective industries.

Testing, Deployment, and Maintenance

In the rapidly evolving world of blockchain technology, testing, deployment, and maintenance play critical roles in ensuring the secure storage and sharing of data. These processes are integral to the successful implementation and long-term viability of blockchain solutions. In this subchapter, we will delve into the importance of testing, deployment, and maintenance in the context of blockchain and its potential impact on various industries.

Testing is a crucial step in the development of any blockchain-based application. It involves rigorous evaluation of the system's functionality, performance, and security. Through comprehensive testing, developers can identify and rectify any vulnerabilities or weaknesses in the blockchain network. This process ensures that the system is robust, reliable, and resistant to potential attacks.

Deployment refers to the process of launching a blockchain solution into a live environment. It involves configuring the system, setting up the necessary infrastructure, and ensuring the smooth integration of the blockchain with existing systems or platforms. Proper deployment is crucial to ensure the effective functioning of the blockchain network and its seamless interaction with other components of the ecosystem.

Maintenance is an ongoing process that ensures the continuous operation and improvement of the blockchain system. It involves monitoring the network, identifying and resolving any issues or bottlenecks, and implementing updates or upgrades as required. Maintenance is essential to keep the blockchain solution up to date with technological advancements and to address any emerging security concerns. Regular maintenance also helps in optimizing the performance and scalability of the system.

For the audience interested in blockchain, understanding the importance of testing, deployment, and maintenance is vital for successful blockchain implementation. Proper testing ensures the reliability and security of the blockchain network, while efficient deployment ensures seamless integration with existing systems. Ongoing maintenance guarantees the long-term viability and effectiveness of the blockchain solution.

Moreover, the niches within the blockchain industry, such as finance, supply chain, healthcare, and governance, require specific considerations during testing, deployment, and maintenance. These niches have unique regulatory requirements, data privacy concerns, and scalability needs. Therefore, developers and organizations working in these niches must tailor their testing, deployment, and maintenance processes to address these specific requirements.

In conclusion, testing, deployment, and maintenance are integral aspects of blockchain implementation. They ensure the security, reliability, and scalability of the system. By following best practices in testing, efficient deployment, and ongoing maintenance, organizations can harness the full potential of blockchain technology for secure data storage and sharing across various industries.

Chapter 7: Case Studies and Real-World Examples

Case Study 1: Blockchain Adoption in a Financial Institution

In this case study, we delve into the real-world application of blockchain technology in a financial institution. As the world embraces the digital age, financial institutions are faced with the challenge of adapting to new technologies while ensuring the security and privacy of their customers' data. Blockchain, with its decentralized and immutable nature, has emerged as a highly promising solution.

The financial institution in focus was grappling with issues such as inefficient and time-consuming processes, lack of transparency, and vulnerability to fraud. Recognizing the potential of blockchain technology, they embarked on a journey to transform their operations.

The first step was to identify the areas where blockchain could bring significant improvements. They began by exploring internal processes, such as cross-border payments, KYC (Know Your Customer) procedures, and document verification. These processes were often plagued by delays, errors, and manual interventions, resulting in increased costs and customer dissatisfaction.

By implementing blockchain, the financial institution successfully streamlined their cross-border payment system. Blockchain's decentralized nature eliminated the need for intermediaries, reducing both costs and processing time. Smart contracts facilitated automatic execution of payments once the predetermined conditions were met, eliminating the need for manual intervention and reducing the risk of errors.

Furthermore, the institution utilized blockchain for KYC procedures and document verification. This eliminated the need for customers to provide the same information repeatedly, as it was securely stored on the blockchain. The tamper-proof nature of the technology ensured the authenticity of documents, reducing the risk of fraud.

By adopting blockchain technology, the financial institution achieved enhanced transparency and security throughout their operations. Customers gained greater control over their data, while the institution experienced increased efficiency and cost savings. The success of this case study has inspired other financial institutions to explore the potential of blockchain technology in their own operations.

This case study serves as a testament to the transformative power of blockchain in the financial sector. As blockchain continues to evolve, financial institutions must embrace this technology to stay ahead in the digital era. By doing so, they can enhance their competitiveness, improve customer satisfaction, and build a more secure and efficient financial ecosystem.

Whether you are an individual seeking to understand the impact of blockchain on the financial industry or a professional looking to implement blockchain solutions in your organization, this case study provides valuable insights into the real-world application of blockchain technology. Join us on this journey to explore the future of data and the role of blockchain in secure storage and sharing.

Case Study 2: Blockchain-powered Healthcare Data Exchange

Introduction:

In recent years, the healthcare industry has witnessed remarkable advancements in technology. One such innovation that has the potential to revolutionize the sector is blockchain. Blockchain technology offers a decentralized and secure way to store and exchange sensitive data, making it an ideal solution for healthcare data management. In this case study, we will explore how blockchain-powered healthcare data exchange can address the challenges faced by the industry and revolutionize patient care.

The Challenges:

In the traditional healthcare system, patient data is scattered across various healthcare providers, making it difficult to access and share crucial information when needed. Additionally, the centralized storage systems are vulnerable to security breaches and data manipulation. These challenges impede seamless collaboration between healthcare providers, leading to delays in diagnosis, treatment, and patient care.

The Blockchain Solution:

Blockchain technology provides a decentralized and immutable ledger that enables secure and transparent data exchange. By leveraging blockchain, healthcare providers can create a unified and interoperable platform for storing and sharing patient data. Each patient's information is securely stored in a blockchain network, ensuring data integrity and privacy. Authorized healthcare professionals can access the patient's medical history, test results, and treatment plans in real-time, leading to faster and more accurate diagnoses.

Benefits and Use Cases:

Blockchain-powered healthcare data exchange offers several benefits. Firstly, patients gain ownership and control over their medical records, allowing them to grant access to different healthcare providers as needed. Secondly, healthcare professionals can make informed decisions based on complete and up-to-date patient information, reducing medical errors and improving patient outcomes. Moreover, blockchain technology can facilitate clinical trials, medical research, and personalized medicine by securely sharing anonymized data.

Real-world examples of blockchain-powered healthcare data exchange are already emerging. For instance, MedRec, a blockchain-based medical record system, enables patients to manage and share their health records with healthcare providers securely. Similarly, Nebula Genomics aims to build a blockchain-based platform that allows individuals to securely store and share their genomic data with researchers, contributing to advancements in precision medicine.

Conclusion:

Blockchain-powered healthcare data exchange has the potential to transform the healthcare industry by providing secure, transparent, and efficient data management solutions. As the technology continues to evolve, it is crucial for healthcare providers, policymakers, and patients to embrace its potential and work together to overcome the challenges associated with implementation. By harnessing the power of blockchain, we can pave the way for a future where patient data is seamlessly shared, leading to improved healthcare outcomes for everyone.

Case Study 3: Blockchain for Supply Chain Transparency

Introduction:

In recent years, the concept of blockchain has gained significant attention, primarily for its potential to revolutionize various industries. One such sector that stands to benefit immensely from blockchain technology is supply chain management. This case study explores the use of blockchain for supply chain transparency, highlighting its advantages, challenges, and real-world applications.

Blockchain for Supply Chain Transparency:

The supply chain is a complex network of multiple entities involved in producing, distributing, and delivering products to consumers. However, this intricate network often faces challenges such as lack of transparency, counterfeiting, and inefficient tracking systems. Blockchain technology offers a promising solution to address these issues.

By leveraging blockchain's decentralized and immutable nature, supply chain participants can record and store every transaction and movement of goods on a shared ledger. This enables real-time visibility and transparency across the entire supply chain, ensuring that every stakeholder has access to accurate and trustworthy information.

Advantages of Blockchain for Supply Chain Transparency:

1. Enhanced Traceability: Blockchain enables end-to-end traceability of products, allowing consumers to verify the origin, journey, and

authenticity of goods. This is particularly crucial in sectors such as food and pharmaceuticals, where safety and quality are paramount.

2. Counterfeit Prevention: Blockchain's tamper-proof nature makes it highly effective in combating counterfeiting. Each product can be assigned a unique digital identity on the blockchain, making it impossible to duplicate or alter without leaving a trace.

3. Efficient Auditing: Traditional auditing processes in supply chains can be time-consuming and prone to errors. By adopting blockchain, auditors can access a transparent and immutable ledger, simplifying the verification of transactions, ensuring compliance, and reducing fraud.

Real-World Applications:

Several companies and organizations have already implemented blockchain for supply chain transparency. For instance, Walmart, one of the world's largest retailers, partnered with IBM to create a blockchain-based food traceability solution. This enables Walmart to track the entire journey of a product, from farm to shelf, ensuring food safety and reducing waste.

In the luxury goods industry, LVMH, a leading conglomerate, is utilizing blockchain to provide proof of authenticity for its high-end products. By integrating a digital certificate on the blockchain, consumers can verify the genuineness of their purchases, reducing the market for counterfeit luxury goods.

Conclusion:

Blockchain technology holds immense potential to transform supply chain management by providing transparency, traceability, and security. The adoption of blockchain in supply chains can lead to improved trust among stakeholders, reduced fraud, and enhanced efficiency. As industries continue to embrace this disruptive technology, the future of supply chain transparency looks promising, benefitting not only businesses but also consumers worldwide.

Case Study 4: Government Records Management

In the digital age, governments worldwide face numerous challenges in managing and securing their vast amounts of records. These records, ranging from citizen information to important documents, are crucial for the effective functioning of governments. However, traditional methods of record-keeping often fall short in terms of security, accessibility, and transparency. This case study explores the potential of blockchain technology in revolutionizing government records management.

Government agencies are responsible for storing and managing an enormous amount of data, including birth and death certificates, property records, tax filings, and more. Not only do these records need to be securely stored, but they must also be easily accessible to authorized individuals. Additionally, ensuring the integrity and authenticity of these records is paramount to maintain public trust.

Blockchain technology offers a promising solution to address these challenges. By its nature, blockchain provides immutability, transparency, and decentralization, making it an ideal platform for storing government records. With blockchain, records can be timestamped, encrypted, and stored in a distributed ledger, making them tamper-resistant and highly secure. This ensures that the data remains intact and untampered with throughout its lifecycle.

Moreover, blockchain allows for improved accessibility and transparency. Authorized individuals can access records securely and efficiently through a decentralized network, eliminating the need for intermediaries and reducing bureaucracy. This not only saves time and resources but also enhances public trust by providing a clear audit trail of the records' history.

One notable example of blockchain implementation in government records management is Estonia's e-Estonia initiative. Estonia has leveraged blockchain technology to create a secure and efficient digital identity system, enabling citizens to access various government services seamlessly. This innovative approach has resulted in improved efficiency, reduced bureaucracy, and increased citizen satisfaction.

While there are challenges to implementing blockchain in government records management, such as scalability and interoperability, the potential benefits are substantial. By embracing blockchain technology, governments can enhance data security, improve accessibility, and strengthen public trust.

In conclusion, government records management is a critical aspect of governance, and traditional methods are often inadequate in the digital age. Blockchain technology offers a promising solution to overcome these challenges by providing a secure, transparent, and decentralized platform for storing and managing government records. Through case studies like Estonia's e-Estonia initiative, it becomes evident that blockchain has the potential to revolutionize government records management, ensuring data integrity, accessibility, and public trust.

Case Study 5: Blockchain-based Education Platform

Introduction:

In this case study, we will explore the innovative use of blockchain technology in the field of education. Blockchain has emerged as a transformative technology with the potential to revolutionize various industries, and education is no exception. This case study focuses on a blockchain-based education platform that harnesses the power of decentralized networks to enhance learning experiences and improve the security and transparency of educational records.

Background:

Traditional education systems often face challenges related to data security, credential verification, and centralized control. These issues can lead to inefficiencies, fraud, and limited access to quality education. However, by leveraging blockchain technology, these problems can be mitigated, offering a promising solution for the future of education.

The Blockchain-based Education Platform:

The blockchain-based education platform discussed in this case study is designed to provide a secure and transparent ecosystem for learners, educators, and institutions. By utilizing a decentralized network, the platform ensures that educational records are tamper-proof and easily verifiable, eliminating the need for intermediaries such as credential evaluators.

Benefits and Features:

1. Enhanced Security: Blockchain's immutable nature ensures that educational records are stored securely, reducing the risk of data breaches or unauthorized modifications. This feature also helps protect the integrity of certificates and diplomas, making them more trustworthy and reliable.

2. Transparent and Traceable Credentials: Through the use of blockchain, learners can have complete control over their educational records, including certificates, achievements, and skills. These credentials can be easily accessed, shared, and verified by potential employers or other educational institutions, increasing transparency and reducing reliance on paper-based documents.

3. Peer-to-Peer Collaboration: The platform fosters a collaborative and decentralized learning environment, allowing learners and educators to connect directly without intermediaries. This enables the exchange of knowledge, ideas, and resources, promoting a more dynamic and interactive learning experience.

4. Access to Global Education: Blockchain technology enables the platform to transcend geographical boundaries, providing learners from all over the world with access to quality education. By removing the need for physical presence, learners can benefit from a diverse range of courses and instructors, expanding their educational opportunities.

Conclusion:

The blockchain-based education platform presented in this case study exemplifies the potential of blockchain technology to revolutionize the field of education. By leveraging the decentralized nature of blockchain, educational systems can overcome challenges related to data security, credential verification, and centralized control. This innovative platform offers enhanced security, transparency, and peer-to-peer collaboration, ultimately empowering learners and educators worldwide. As blockchain continues to evolve, its impact on education is likely to be transformative, paving the way for a more inclusive and efficient learning ecosystem for everyone.

Chapter 8: Future Possibilities and Potential Disruptions

Exploring Emerging Technologies and Trends

In today's rapidly evolving digital landscape, the exploration of emerging technologies and trends is crucial for individuals and businesses alike. One such technology that has gained significant attention is blockchain. This revolutionary technology has the potential to transform various industries, including finance, healthcare, supply chain management, and more.

Blockchain is a distributed ledger technology that enables secure and transparent transactions without the need for intermediaries. It works by creating a decentralized network of computers, also known as nodes, that collectively validate and record transactions in a chronological order. This makes the data stored on a blockchain highly secure and resistant to tampering.

The potential applications of blockchain technology are vast. For instance, in the financial sector, blockchain can streamline cross-border payments, reduce transaction costs, and enhance transparency. It can also facilitate the creation of digital identities, ensuring secure and verifiable online interactions. Additionally, blockchain can revolutionize supply chain management by providing real-time tracking of goods, reducing fraud, and improving overall efficiency.

As blockchain technology continues to gain traction, it is essential to stay up-to-date with the latest trends. One emerging trend is the integration of blockchain with other technologies such as artificial intelligence (AI) and the Internet of Things (IoT). This convergence can create powerful solutions that leverage the strengths of each technology, leading to improved efficiency and innovation.

Moreover, the rise of decentralized finance (DeFi) is another trend worth exploring. DeFi refers to the use of blockchain technology and smart contracts to recreate traditional financial instruments, such as lending and borrowing, in a decentralized manner. This allows for greater financial inclusion, as individuals can access financial services without the need for traditional intermediaries.

In conclusion, understanding and exploring emerging technologies and trends, particularly in the realm of blockchain, is crucial for individuals and businesses in today's digital age. Blockchain has the potential to revolutionize various industries, and staying informed about its applications and the latest trends can provide a competitive edge. Whether you are a technology enthusiast, a business owner, or simply curious about the future of data, delving into the world of blockchain and its emerging technologies is an exciting and essential journey to embark on.

Impact of Artificial Intelligence and Internet of Things

Artificial Intelligence (AI) and the Internet of Things (IoT) are two groundbreaking technologies that have the potential to revolutionize various industries and transform the way we live and work. In this subchapter, we will explore the impact of AI and IoT on the blockchain technology and discuss the potential benefits and challenges they present to the future of data storage and sharing.

The convergence of AI and IoT has the power to create an interconnected network of devices and systems that can collect and analyze vast amounts of data in real-time. This data can be used to derive valuable insights, improve decision-making processes, and enhance operational efficiency. With the integration of blockchain technology, this data can be securely stored and shared, ensuring transparency, immutability, and accountability.

One of the significant impacts of AI and IoT on the blockchain is the ability to create a more decentralized and secure network. Traditional centralized systems are vulnerable to hacking and data breaches, but with the use of blockchain, data is distributed across multiple nodes, making it nearly impossible for hackers to alter or manipulate the information. This enhanced security can revolutionize industries such as finance, healthcare, supply chain, and energy, where data privacy and integrity are of utmost importance.

Moreover, AI can leverage the data gathered from IoT devices to create intelligent algorithms that can autonomously make decisions and perform tasks. This can lead to automation and optimization of various processes, reducing human error and increasing productivity.

For instance, in the healthcare sector, AI-powered IoT devices can monitor patients' vital signs and automatically alert healthcare providers in case of any abnormality, enabling swift medical interventions and potentially saving lives.

However, the integration of AI and IoT with blockchain also brings challenges that need to be addressed. The sheer volume of data generated by IoT devices combined with the complexity of AI algorithms can strain the scalability and performance of blockchain networks. Additionally, ensuring privacy while maintaining transparency and complying with data protection regulations is a delicate balance that needs to be achieved.

In conclusion, the impact of AI and IoT on the blockchain technology is immense and holds tremendous potential for the future of data storage and sharing. By combining these technologies, we can create a more secure, efficient, and transparent ecosystem that empowers individuals and organizations alike. However, it is crucial to address the challenges to fully harness the benefits of this convergence. The future of data in the blockchain era is undoubtedly exciting, and it is up to us to explore and leverage the potential of AI and IoT to shape a better world for everyone.

Interplay between Blockchain and Other Technologies

Blockchain technology has emerged as a transformative force that is revolutionizing industries across the globe. However, its true potential can be fully realized when combined with other complementary technologies. In this subchapter, we delve into the interplay between blockchain and other groundbreaking technologies, exploring the synergies they create and the possibilities they unlock.

One of the key technologies that seamlessly integrates with blockchain is the Internet of Things (IoT). The IoT enables the connection of physical devices through the internet, facilitating the exchange of data and triggering actions between these devices. By integrating blockchain with IoT, we can ensure the secure and transparent exchange of data, eliminating the need for intermediaries and enhancing data integrity. This convergence enables us to create trustless and autonomous systems that can be applied in various sectors, from supply chain management to smart cities.

Artificial Intelligence (AI) is another technology that beautifully complements blockchain. AI algorithms can analyze vast amounts of data and make intelligent decisions. When combined with blockchain's decentralized nature, AI can provide valuable insights into data patterns and trends, leading to more accurate predictions and improved decision-making processes. Additionally, blockchain can enhance the transparency and accountability of AI systems, mitigating concerns around biased or unethical algorithms.

Cloud computing is yet another technology that can benefit from blockchain integration. The decentralized nature of blockchain can enhance the security and privacy of cloud-based services, reducing the risk of data breaches and unauthorized access. By leveraging blockchain's distributed ledger, cloud storage providers can offer enhanced data integrity, ensuring that data remains tamper-proof and verifiable.

Moreover, blockchain and virtual reality (VR) can create exciting possibilities. VR can provide immersive experiences, while blockchain can ensure the ownership and provenance of virtual assets. By combining these technologies, we can create virtual worlds with secure and transparent economies, where users can confidently buy, sell, and trade virtual assets, knowing that their ownership rights are protected.

In conclusion, the interplay between blockchain and other technologies is unlocking a vast array of possibilities. From IoT and AI to cloud computing and VR, blockchain integration enhances the security, transparency, and trustworthiness of these technologies. This convergence is reshaping industries, enabling new business models, and transforming the way we store, share, and analyze data. By embracing this interplay, we can pave the way for a future where blockchain is at the core of a secure, interconnected, and decentralized digital ecosystem.

Disruptive Potential of Blockchain in Various Industries

Blockchain technology has emerged as a game-changer in today's digital landscape, offering unprecedented opportunities for innovation and transformation across various industries. Its decentralized and immutable nature has the potential to revolutionize the way we conduct business, store data, and ensure trust and security in transactions. In this subchapter, we will delve into the disruptive potential of blockchain in various industries and how it is poised to reshape the future.

1. Finance and Banking:
The financial industry stands to benefit immensely from blockchain's transparency, security, and efficiency. Blockchain-powered smart contracts can automate complex financial transactions while eliminating the need for intermediaries, reducing costs, and increasing trust. Additionally, blockchain can streamline identity verification, reduce fraud, and enable seamless cross-border transactions.

2. Supply Chain Management:
Blockchain technology can revolutionize supply chain management by providing end-to-end transparency and traceability. With blockchain, stakeholders can track the movement of goods from raw materials to the end consumer, ensuring authenticity, preventing counterfeit products, and improving efficiency. This technology can also enhance compliance with regulations and enable faster dispute resolution.

3. Healthcare:
Healthcare is another industry that can greatly benefit from blockchain's disruptive potential. Blockchain can enable secure and

interoperable health records, ensuring privacy and data integrity. It can also facilitate the secure sharing of medical data, leading to better collaboration among healthcare providers, more accurate diagnoses, and improved patient care.

4. Real Estate:
Blockchain has the potential to revolutionize the real estate industry by simplifying property transactions and reducing fraud. Smart contracts can automate property transfers, ensuring faster and more secure transactions. Blockchain can also enable fractional ownership and tokenization, making real estate investments more accessible and liquid.

5. Energy:
Blockchain technology can disrupt the energy sector by enabling peer-to-peer energy trading and decentralized energy grids. With blockchain, consumers can directly buy and sell excess energy, reducing reliance on centralized energy providers. This can lead to a more efficient and sustainable energy ecosystem.

6. Education:
Blockchain can transform the education industry by providing secure and verifiable credentials. With blockchain-based certificates and degrees, employers can easily verify the authenticity of an individual's qualifications, reducing the risk of credential fraud. This technology can also facilitate lifelong learning and the recognition of informal education.

In conclusion, blockchain technology has the potential to disrupt various industries, offering enhanced security, transparency, efficiency, and trust. Its decentralized and immutable nature has the power to reshape traditional business models, streamline processes, and create new opportunities. As blockchain continues to evolve, it is essential for businesses and individuals to embrace its potential and explore innovative use cases to stay ahead in this rapidly changing digital landscape.

Chapter 9: Overcoming Challenges and Adoption Barriers

Addressing Security and Privacy Concerns

In the ever-evolving digital landscape, security and privacy concerns have become paramount. With the rise of blockchain technology, however, there is hope for a more secure and private future. This subchapter delves into the crucial topic of addressing security and privacy concerns within the blockchain ecosystem.

Blockchain technology offers a decentralized and immutable ledger that ensures transparency and security. By employing cryptographic techniques, blockchain eliminates the need for intermediaries, making it inherently resistant to tampering and fraud. This feature alone makes blockchain an ideal solution for addressing security concerns in various industries, including finance, healthcare, and supply chain management.

One of the primary security benefits of blockchain lies in its consensus mechanism. By reaching a consensus among multiple nodes, blockchain ensures that any changes made to the data are validated and approved by the network. This decentralized approach significantly reduces the risk of data breaches or unauthorized access. Additionally, the use of encryption techniques in blockchain further enhances data security, making it nearly impossible for malicious actors to decrypt sensitive information.

Privacy concerns have also been a growing issue in the digital age. With personal data being collected and stored by various organizations, individuals are rightly concerned about the misuse or unauthorized access to their information. Blockchain technology can offer a solution to these concerns by providing a more secure and private method of data storage and sharing.

Blockchain's architecture allows for the creation of private and permissioned networks, ensuring that only authorized participants have access to sensitive data. This feature is particularly valuable in industries where data privacy is of utmost importance, such as healthcare or personal finance. Moreover, blockchain's decentralized nature eliminates the need for a trusted third party, reducing the risk of data breaches or leaks.

However, it is important to note that while blockchain technology provides enhanced security and privacy, it is not a silver bullet. Like any technology, it has its limitations and vulnerabilities. It is crucial for organizations and individuals to understand these limitations and implement additional security measures to safeguard their data effectively.

In conclusion, blockchain technology has the potential to revolutionize the way we address security and privacy concerns. By leveraging its decentralized and immutable nature, blockchain provides a robust solution to combat data breaches and unauthorized access. As the technology continues to evolve, it is essential for organizations and individuals to stay informed and proactive in addressing security and privacy concerns within the blockchain ecosystem. Only through collective efforts and continuous improvement can we ensure a secure and private future for all.

Educating and Creating Awareness among Stakeholders

In the rapidly evolving landscape of blockchain technology, it is crucial to educate and create awareness among stakeholders. Blockchain, with its decentralized and transparent nature, has the potential to revolutionize various industries and transform the way we store and share data securely. This subchapter aims to explore the importance of educating individuals from all walks of life about blockchain and its role in secure storage and sharing.

Blockchain technology is not limited to a particular niche or industry; it has the potential to impact everyone. Whether you are a student, a business owner, a healthcare professional, or a government official, understanding blockchain can be beneficial in several ways. By creating awareness among stakeholders, we can ensure that everyone is equipped with the knowledge to harness the power of blockchain and make informed decisions.

For individuals, understanding blockchain opens up new opportunities. It allows for secure and transparent transactions, eliminates the need for intermediaries, and provides control over personal data. By educating individuals about blockchain, we empower them to protect their privacy and make better-informed decisions when using blockchain-based platforms or services.

Businesses, both large and small, can benefit greatly from embracing blockchain technology. Educating stakeholders about blockchain can help them understand how it can streamline their operations, increase efficiency, and reduce costs. From supply chain management to identity verification, blockchain has the potential to revolutionize various aspects of business operations. By creating awareness, businesses can stay ahead of the curve and tap into the potential of blockchain.

In the healthcare industry, educating stakeholders about blockchain can pave the way for secure and interoperable health records. Blockchain can enhance data security, enable accurate patient identification, and facilitate efficient data sharing between healthcare providers. By spreading awareness about blockchain's role in healthcare, we can drive the adoption of this transformative technology and improve patient outcomes.

Government officials and policymakers also play a crucial role in the adoption and regulation of blockchain technology. Educating them about blockchain's potential can help create a conducive environment for innovation, ensuring that regulations are balanced and do not stifle growth. By understanding blockchain's capabilities, government entities can explore its applications in areas like voting systems, land registries, and public service delivery.

Educating and creating awareness among stakeholders is essential to unlock the full potential of blockchain technology. By equipping individuals, businesses, and government entities with the knowledge to harness blockchain's capabilities, we can build a more secure, transparent, and efficient future. This subchapter aims to provide insights and resources for every individual, regardless of their background or industry, to understand and embrace the future of data powered by blockchain.

Regulatory Frameworks and Compliance

In the fast-paced world of blockchain technology, it is crucial to have a solid understanding of the regulatory frameworks and compliance measures that govern its usage. As blockchain continues to revolutionize various industries, it becomes essential for both businesses and individuals to navigate these frameworks to ensure security, transparency, and compliance.

Regulatory frameworks for blockchain technology vary across different countries and jurisdictions, making it imperative to stay up-to-date with the latest developments. Governments are increasingly recognizing the potential of blockchain and are taking steps to establish guidelines and regulations that promote responsible use while protecting the interests of users.

One of the key aspects of regulatory frameworks for blockchain is the identification and verification of participants. Due to the decentralized nature of blockchain, traditional identity verification methods may not apply. Governments and regulatory bodies are exploring innovative ways to address this challenge, such as digital identity solutions and self-sovereign identity models. These solutions aim to strike a balance between privacy and security, enabling individuals to maintain control over their personal information while complying with regulatory requirements.

Another vital aspect of compliance in blockchain is data protection and privacy. With the increasing amount of personal and sensitive data being stored on blockchain networks, it is crucial to establish robust data protection measures. Regulatory frameworks often include provisions for encryption, data access controls, and secure storage mechanisms to ensure the privacy and integrity of information.

Smart contracts, an integral part of blockchain technology, also require regulatory attention. These self-executing contracts are governed by predetermined rules and conditions, but there is a need to ensure that these rules comply with existing legal frameworks. Governments are actively exploring ways to integrate smart contracts into existing legal systems and establish a legal framework that supports their enforcement.

In addition to government regulations, compliance with industry standards and best practices is essential for organizations operating in the blockchain space. Organizations must adhere to established standards to ensure interoperability, security, and trust among stakeholders. Compliance with these standards not only enhances the credibility of blockchain solutions but also fosters collaboration and innovation within the industry.

As blockchain technology continues to evolve, so will the regulatory frameworks and compliance measures surrounding it. It is essential for all stakeholders, whether businesses or individuals, to stay informed and adapt to these changes. By understanding and complying with regulatory frameworks, we can harness the full potential of blockchain technology while ensuring its responsible and secure usage.

In conclusion, regulatory frameworks and compliance play a vital role in shaping the future of blockchain technology. They provide a framework for addressing identity verification, data protection, and privacy concerns, as well as ensuring the enforcement of smart contracts. Adhering to these frameworks and industry standards is crucial for organizations operating in the blockchain space to foster trust, collaboration, and innovation. As blockchain technology continues to disrupt various industries, it is imperative for everyone to stay informed and navigate these regulatory frameworks to ensure secure storage and sharing of data.

Interoperability and Standardization Efforts

One of the most significant challenges facing the blockchain industry is the lack of interoperability and standardization. As the technology continues to evolve and gain traction across various sectors, the need for seamless integration and standardized protocols becomes increasingly crucial. This subchapter explores the ongoing efforts in the blockchain community to address these issues and the potential benefits of achieving interoperability and standardization.

Interoperability refers to the ability of different blockchain networks to communicate and share data seamlessly. Currently, most blockchains operate in isolation, making it difficult for them to interact with each other. This lack of interoperability limits the potential applications of blockchain technology, as it hinders the efficient transfer of assets and data across different networks. To overcome this challenge, several initiatives are underway to develop protocols and frameworks that enable interoperability between blockchains.

Standardization, on the other hand, involves the establishment of uniform rules and protocols for blockchain development and implementation. In the absence of standardized practices, the blockchain ecosystem becomes fragmented, making it difficult for businesses and individuals to adopt the technology with confidence. Standardization efforts aim to create a common set of rules that facilitate collaboration, compatibility, and scalability across different blockchain platforms.

Several organizations and consortiums are actively working towards achieving interoperability and standardization in the blockchain industry. For example, the InterWork Alliance (IWA) is a global consortium that focuses on developing standards and frameworks for tokenization and asset interoperability. Their efforts aim to enable seamless transfer of digital assets across different blockchain networks, promoting a more efficient and interconnected ecosystem.

Another notable initiative is the Blockchain Interoperability Alliance (BIA), which brings together blockchain projects and industry leaders to collaborate on interoperability solutions. Through research, development, and advocacy, the BIA seeks to establish common standards and protocols that enable cross-chain communication and interoperability.

The benefits of achieving interoperability and standardization in the blockchain industry are numerous. It would allow for the seamless transfer of assets, data, and value across different networks, unlocking new possibilities for collaboration and innovation. Standardization would also foster trust and confidence in the technology, making it easier for businesses and individuals to adopt blockchain solutions. Furthermore, interoperability and standardization could pave the way for the creation of decentralized applications (dApps) that can operate across multiple blockchains, enhancing scalability and usability.

In conclusion, interoperability and standardization efforts are crucial for the future of blockchain technology. By enabling seamless communication and establishing common rules, the industry can overcome its current limitations and unlock the full potential of blockchain. Collaboration among organizations and consortiums is essential to drive these efforts forward and ensure the widespread adoption of blockchain across different sectors.

Chapter 10: Conclusion and Looking Ahead

Recap of Key Learnings

As we come to the end of our journey exploring the future of data and blockchain's role in secure storage and sharing, it is important to recap some of the key learnings we have gained. Throughout this book, we have delved into the intricacies of blockchain technology and its potential to revolutionize the way we handle and protect data.

First and foremost, we have established that blockchain is not limited to cryptocurrencies like Bitcoin. It is a decentralized ledger that can securely store and verify transactions or any type of data. This opens up a world of possibilities for industries beyond finance, as blockchain can provide an immutable, transparent, and tamper-proof system for data management.

One of the most significant advantages of blockchain technology is its ability to enhance security. By utilizing cryptographic algorithms and distributed consensus mechanisms, blockchain ensures that data remains secure and tamper-resistant. This is particularly crucial in an era where data breaches and cyberattacks are becoming increasingly common.

Furthermore, blockchain enables enhanced data privacy and ownership. Traditional centralized systems often give organizations control over user data, leading to concerns about privacy and misuse. With blockchain, individuals can have greater control over their own data, determining who has access to it and how it is utilized, thereby fostering a more transparent and fair digital environment.

Another key learning is that blockchain offers increased efficiency and cost savings. By eliminating intermediaries and automating processes, blockchain can streamline various operations, reducing time, effort, and expenses. This promises to revolutionize supply chains, healthcare systems, government processes, and many other sectors that rely on complex data management.

Lastly, we have explored the challenges and limitations of blockchain technology. Scalability, energy consumption, regulatory concerns, and the need for interoperability are among the hurdles that need to be overcome for widespread adoption. However, it is important to note that these challenges are not insurmountable, and ongoing research and development are continuously addressing these issues.

In conclusion, the future of data is closely intertwined with blockchain technology. By embracing the decentralized nature of blockchain, we can create a more secure, transparent, and efficient digital ecosystem. Whether you are a blockchain enthusiast, a professional in the tech industry, or simply someone curious about the potential of blockchain, understanding these key learnings will enable you to navigate the ever-evolving landscape of data storage and sharing with confidence and insight.

Future Outlook for Blockchain in Secure Data Storage and Sharing

In recent years, blockchain technology has emerged as a game-changer in various industries. Its decentralized nature and cryptographic algorithms have made it a highly secure platform for data storage and sharing. As we look towards the future, the potential of blockchain in secure data storage and sharing is immense, promising a revolution in how we protect and exchange information.

One of the key advantages of blockchain technology lies in its ability to provide tamper-proof and transparent data storage. Traditional centralized databases are vulnerable to hacking and data breaches, as they rely on a single point of failure. Blockchain, on the other hand, is a distributed ledger that stores data across a network of computers, making it nearly impossible for hackers to compromise the system. This decentralized architecture ensures data integrity and enhances security, making it an ideal solution for sensitive information storage.

Moreover, blockchain offers enhanced privacy and control over data. With traditional systems, individuals often have to trust third parties to safeguard their data. However, blockchain eliminates the need for intermediaries, allowing users to have full control over their information. By employing encryption techniques and smart contracts, blockchain ensures that data is accessible only to authorized individuals, reducing the risk of unauthorized access and data misuse.

The future of blockchain in secure data storage and sharing holds immense potential. As blockchain technology matures, we can expect to see increased adoption in industries such as healthcare, finance, and supply chain management. For instance, in the healthcare sector, blockchain can enable secure and interoperable sharing of patient records among different providers, improving the quality of care and reducing medical errors. Similarly, in finance, blockchain can streamline the process of cross-border transactions, eliminating the need for intermediaries and reducing costs.

Furthermore, blockchain can revolutionize intellectual property rights and digital content distribution. By leveraging blockchain's decentralized nature, artists and content creators can have greater control over their work, ensuring fair compensation and protection against piracy. This can lead to a more equitable and transparent digital economy.

In conclusion, the future outlook for blockchain in secure data storage and sharing is incredibly promising. The technology's inherent security, transparency, and privacy features make it a powerful tool for protecting sensitive information and enabling secure data exchange. As industries recognize the potential benefits of blockchain, we can expect widespread adoption and innovation in the coming years. By embracing blockchain technology, we can usher in a new era of secure and trusted data storage and sharing for everyone.

Final Thoughts and Recommendations for Readers

In this book, we have embarked on a journey to explore the future of data and the crucial role that blockchain technology plays in secure storage and sharing. We have delved into the depths of blockchain's potential, its impact on various industries, and how it can revolutionize the way we handle data.

As we conclude this book, it is important to reflect on the key takeaways and provide you, the reader, with some final thoughts and recommendations.

Firstly, it is evident that blockchain technology has the power to transform the way we store and share data. Its decentralized nature ensures that no single entity has complete control, eliminating the need for intermediaries and reducing the risk of data breaches. As a reader interested in the blockchain field, it is crucial to stay updated with the latest advancements, as this technology continues to evolve rapidly.

Secondly, the potential applications of blockchain go far beyond cryptocurrency. We have explored its impact on healthcare, supply chain management, finance, and even voting systems. It is clear that blockchain has the capacity to create more transparent, efficient, and secure processes in various sectors. As a reader, we encourage you to explore these applications further and identify opportunities for innovation within your own niche.

Furthermore, as blockchain technology evolves, so do the challenges associated with it. Scalability, energy consumption, and regulatory frameworks are just a few of the hurdles that need to be addressed. To overcome these challenges, collaboration and interdisciplinary efforts are necessary. We recommend engaging in forums, conferences, and communities dedicated to blockchain and data security, as they offer valuable insights and opportunities for networking with like-minded individuals.

Lastly, we emphasize the importance of education and awareness. Blockchain technology is still relatively nascent, and its concepts can be complex to grasp. Educating yourself and others about the fundamentals of blockchain, its benefits, and its potential risks will contribute to its widespread adoption and successful implementation.

In conclusion, the future of data lies in the hands of blockchain technology. Its potential to revolutionize industries and enhance data security is unparalleled. By staying informed, exploring its applications, collaborating, and fostering awareness, we can collectively drive the adoption of blockchain and pave the way for a more secure and efficient digital future.

Remember, the power of blockchain is in the hands of every individual, and it is up to us to harness this technology to shape a better tomorrow.

www.ingramcontent.com/pod-product-compliance
Lightning Source LLC
Chambersburg PA
CBHW071541150726
48000CB00002B/886
* 9 7 9 8 8 6 9 0 4 9 0 2 5 *